Row, Row, Row the Boats

A Fun Song About George Washington Crossing the Delaware

By Michael Dahl   Illustrated by Sandra D'Antonio

Special thanks to our advisers for their expertise:

Tom Mega, Ph.D., Department of History
University of St. Thomas (Minnesota)

Susan Kesselring, M.A., Literacy Educat
Rosemount-Apple Valley-Eagan (Minne

PICTURE WINDOW BOOKS
MINNEAPOLIS, MINNESOTA

Managing Editor: Bob Temple
Creative Director: Terri Foley
Editor: Kristin Thoennes Keller
Editorial Adviser: Andrea Cascardi
Copy Editor: Laurie Kahn
Musical arrangement: Elizabeth Temple
Designer: Melissa Voda
Page production: The Design Lab
The illustrations in this book were created digitally.

Picture Window Books

5115 Excelsior Boulevard
Suite 232
Minneapolis, MN 55416
1-877-845-8392
www.picturewindowbooks.com

Printed in the United States of America.

Library of Congress Cataloging-in-Publication Data
Dahl, Michael.
Row, row, row the boats : a fun song about George Washington crossing the Delaware /
Michael Dahl ; illustrator, Sandra D'Antonio.
p. cm. — (Fun songs)
Summary: Relates the Revolutionary War adventures of George Washington as he led his troops
toward the Battle of Trenton, interspersed with verses of original song lyrics to be sung to the tune
of "Row, Row, Row Your Boat." Includes bibliographical references (p.) and index.
ISBN 1-4048-0128-6 (lib. bdg.)
1. Trenton, Battle of, Trenton, N.J., 1776—Juvenile literature. 2. Trenton, Battle of, Trenton, N.J.,
1776—Songs and music—Juvenile literature. 3. Washington, George, 1732-1799—Juvenile
literature. 4. Washington, George, 1732-1799—Songs and music—Juvenile literature. [1. Trenton,
Battle of, Trenton, N.J., 1776. 2. Washington, George, 1732-1799. 3. United States—History—
Revolution, 1775-1783—Campaigns. 4. Trenton, Battle of, Trenton, N.J., 1776—Songs and music.
5. Washington, George, 1732-1799—Songs and music. 6. United States—History—Revolution,
1775-1783—Songs and music.] I. D'Antonio, Sandra, 1956- ill. II. Title.
E241.T7 D34 2004
973.3'32—dc21   2003009836

SING ONE! SING ALL!
It's the new historical ditty:
"Row, Row, Row the Boats."

Sing along to the tune of "Row, Row, Row Your Boat."
Tell the tale of George Washington
and his cold soldiers at the Battle of Trenton!

Long ago, America was not a country. People who lived there were called colonists. They were ruled by the King of Great Britain. He made the colonists pay money called taxes. Many colonists wanted their freedom from Britain. They called themselves patriots. They fought British troops for their freedom.

George Washington led the patriot army. It was a big job. British troops were the strongest in the world. George's troops were not trained soldiers. They didn't have as many supplies as the British did.

The patriot soldiers grew discouraged. Many left the army. They returned to their homes. George needed a victory after losing a big battle in New York. He wanted to give his troops hope. The fight for freedom would be lost if they quit too soon. Then George got a great idea. This song tells the story of George's victory at Trenton.

Row, row, row the boats!
Cross the Delaware!

George's troops were outdoors on Christmas night in 1775. It was freezing cold. George wanted to cross the Delaware River for a surprise attack on the other side.

5

Washington and his two thousand men will fight the Hessians there.

Hessians were German soldiers that the British had hired to fight for them. The Hessian leader did not send anyone to guard the river that night because the weather was bad.

Snow, snow, snow and ice blow against the boats.

A blizzard of snow and sleet fell that night. Chunks of thick ice banged against the boats.

9

Washington and his two thousand men are freezing in their coats.

Some soldiers did not have boots. They wrapped old blankets around their feet. Others went barefoot in the snow.

Blow, blow, blow the winds.
Sleet is raining down.

Washington and his two thousand men march on to Trenton town.

George's troops were tired after crossing the river. George let them rest for an hour. They still had nearly 10 miles (16 kilometers) ahead of them.

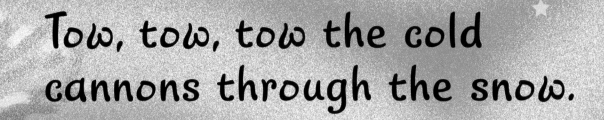

Tow, tow, tow the cold cannons through the snow.

The patriots brought 18 cannons across the river. It was lucky they did. Many guns did not work. They were soaked with rain and snow. But the cannons still fired.

Washington and his two thousand men surprise their sleeping foe.

Rows, rows, rows of men
run through Trenton town.

Washington and his two thousand men have won this one, hands down!

The fight with the Hessians lasted about 45 minutes. The victory gave hope to George's troops. It also gave hope to other patriots in the land.

Row, Row, Row the Boats

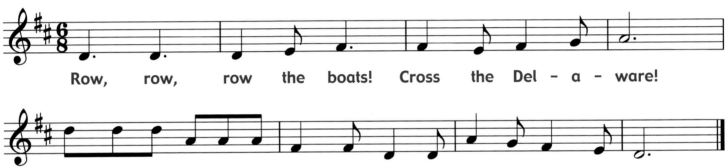

Row, row, row the boats! Cross the Del – a – ware!

Wash – ing – ton and his two thou – sand men will fight the Hes – sians there.

2. Snow, snow, snow and ice
Blow against the boats.
Washington and his two thousand men
Are freezing in their coats.

3. Blow, blow, blow the winds.
Sleet is raining down.
Washington and his two thousand men
March on to Trenton town.

4. Tow, tow, tow the cold
Cannons through the snow.
Washington and his two thousand men
Surprise their sleeping foe.

5. Rows, rows, rows of men
Run through Trenton town.
Washington and his two thousand men
Have won this one, hands down!

Did You Know?

Did you know that George Washington was in pain during the war?
George had bad teeth. One by one, they broke off or fell out.
George's dentist made false teeth for him. They were made
from cow's teeth, human teeth, and elephant ivory.
They fit poorly and caused him pain. They also changed
the shape of his mouth.

Did you know that George Washington
was a smart leader in war?
George often fooled the British troops.
He planned surprise attacks. Once, he moved
his army by night but left campfires burning.
The British did not know his army had moved.
George also fooled the British about the size
of his troops. He had spies in the British army.
George told the spies to say his army
was bigger than it really was.

GLOSSARY

cannon—a large gun that fires heavy metal balls

Hessian—a German soldier hired by the British

patriot—a person who loves and fights for his or her country

sleet—rain that is partly frozen

tax—money that people pay to their government

23

To Learn More

AT THE LIBRARY

Chandra, Deborah, and Madeleine Comora. *George Washington's Teeth.* New York: Farrar Straus Giroux, 2003.

Thoennes Keller, Kristin. *George Washington.* Mankato, Minn.: Bridgestone Books, 2002.

Tucker, Mary. *Washington Crossing the Delaware: History—Hands On.* Carthage, Ill.: Teaching & Learning Co., 2002.

ON THE WEB

Washington Crossing State Park

http://www.state.nj.us/dep/forestry/parks/washcros.htm

Shows the site where Washington and his troops crossed the river

Fact Monster: American Revolution

http://www.factmonster.com/ce6/history/A0803694.html

Explains the American Revolution to kids

Fact Hound

Fact Hound offers a safe, fun way to find Web sites related to this book.
All of the sites on Fact Hound have been researched by our staff.
http://www.facthound.com

1. Visit the Fact Hound home page.
2. Enter a search word related to this book
   or type in this special code: 1404801286.
3. Click on the FETCH IT button.

Your trusty Fact Hound will fetch the best sites for you!